ART AND THE MONAD

ART AND THE MONAD

Keith Lincoln Cook

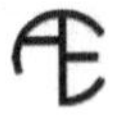

Published by AoE Publishing 2016

First published in Australia in
2016 by
AoE Publishing
Sydney, Australia

ISBN: 978-0-9873473-5-0
Printed and bound by LSI

Photograph of Keith Lincoln Cook by Andris Abolins
Photograph on back cover by Keith Lincoln Cook

FOREWORD

In April 2016, Keith contacted me and asked if I would be willing to help him with an essay on art and the monad. He remarked that the subject was one he had been talking and writing about since the early 1980s, but during all that time he had been unable to pull his ideas together into a compact entity. Also, at the end of January 2016, he had lost 75% of his sight, and the possibility of the project ever being completed had become extremely unlikely.

I agreed to help him, and after listening while he presented his ideas I read through his many writings on the subject. Finally I merged everything into what became *Art and the Monad*. Although his blindness has restricted him in obvious ways, he once remarked that it had actually helped intensify his understanding of the concepts behind his thinking. 'I've observed so much about people since I've become blind,' he said, 'things that I'd never observed before.'

Keith's diagram of his monad is central to the ideas presented in this essay – ideas concerning the importance of being able to experience unobstructed emotional responses to external stimuli, especially in regards to art. It is to be hoped that both his diagram and the related ideas will provoke thought and discussion. This, after all, is the purpose of the essay.

Finally, being able to respond freely to everything around us, not only art, should be a goal worth aspiring to, regardless of who we are or how we think.

Diane Eklund-Āboliņš
June, 2016

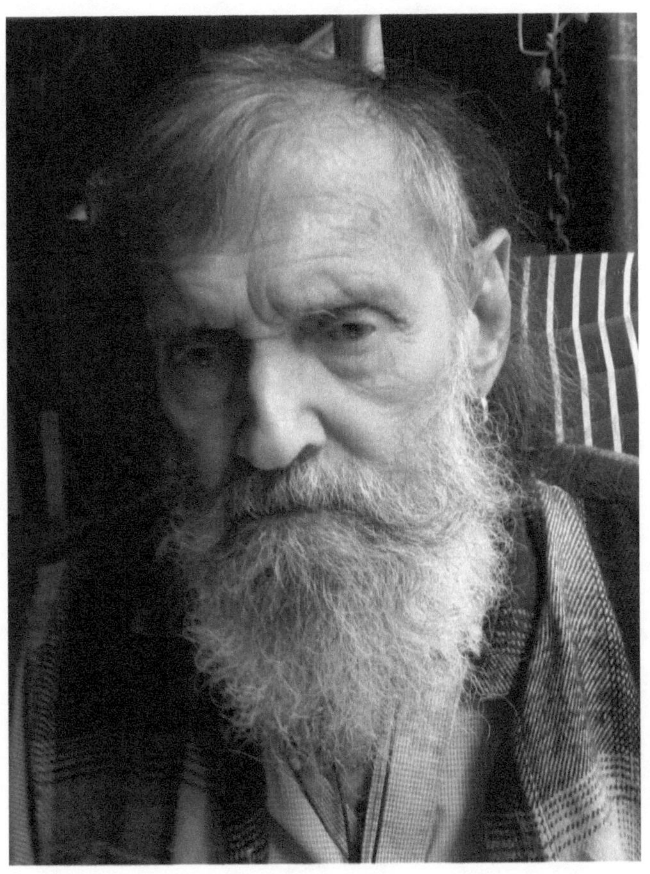

Yesterday's novelty
Today's recluse
Tomorrow's deceased

ART AND THE MONAD

THE MONAD

What, you may well ask, is a monad? According to the Oxford Reference Dictionary[1], a monad is defined as: *n.* **1** the number one; a unit. **2** *Philos.* any ultimate unit of being (e.g. a soul, an atom, a person, God). **3** *Biol.* a simple organism, e.g. one assumed as the first in the genealogy of human beings.

The word monad is also found in the word monadelphous, *Bot.* which refers to the filaments of stamens being bundled together into one unit or whole. No matter the definition, the word conjures

---

1   Judy Pearsall & Bill Trumble, editors, *The Oxford Reference Dictionary*, Oxford: Oxford University Press, 1995

up the image of a unit or a totality. This is the idea at the centre of *my* monad, which is simply a symbol for the completeness or the integrity of man's mind and emotions.

At the end of 1979, I was living in Townsville and my life had reached what is best described as a dead end. Consequently, when I applied for a position on Thursday Island as a liaison officer with the Department of Foreign Affairs, I was fervently hoping that, were I to be successful, the change of scene and direction could be the catalyst I needed to turn my life around.

While my application was still being considered, I flew up to assess the place: a small island in the Torres Strait, about forty kilometres north of Cape York. It did not, however, take long for me to ascertain that, in spite of its colour and its singularity, Thursday Island had very little to offer me as a single male person. Quickly realizing that should I be offered the position I would be unable to accept it, I was faced with the unwelcome truth that I was more or less back at square one: I still had no idea how to extricate myself from the very depressed and stagnant situation in which I had been floundering for some time.

I remained on the island for several weeks, living in a dingy hotel while trying to decide on my next move. As far as I could see, my life had come to a complete standstill: I had exhausted all my available capital and, in moments of melancholy, I easily convinced myself that I had achieved nothing in almost fifty years of life. Enveloped by the heavy, tropical heat, I spent many hours reflecting on what it was that had actually landed me in such a predicament and what I should do to disentangle myself from it; I also spent much time writing about my life up to that point. No doubt I was hoping that the physical exercise of putting pen to paper would help me clarify my ideas and illuminate a solution to my present situation. In an outpouring of words on many handwritten pages, I explored my childhood, my adulthood, my relationships and my careers, and gradually came to realize that all the most important events in my life were in some way intertwined with the visual arts.

I finally left Thursday Island and went to Cairns where, after surviving several weeks in yet another dingy hotel, I moved into a rooming house. It was at this point that I bought my first typewriter and began developing many of the ideas that had come into being, during my time on Thursday Island. Having navigated my way on to a new path, I was aware that the weeks of self-examination had given rise to a myriad of ideas and observations. One thought that kept pushing to the surface concerned the obviously strong connection between my most important achievements and the visual arts, and it ultimately occurred to me that during my time as an art teacher, and later during the period I was managing my own commercial arts studio, all my success was most probably thanks to an innate awareness of the very essence of art – an essence which I define as an emotional or spiritual response to external stimuli.

With many new friends, an inspiring social and intellectual life and a complete change of career as a handyman, I discovered Cairns to be the catalyst for which I had been searching. My thoughts, which had been exceptionally bleak during my stay on Thursday Island, were finally moving into more positive territory.

Besides the understanding concerning my different achievements, there was yet another idea that emerged during the weeks of introspection. It was one that continued to intrigue me, and it concerned our patterns of thinking and acting. I spent much time trying to determine what actually goes on in people's minds, including my own, and why we act the way we do. To a certain degree this speculation was instigated by issues I had had with certain people in the past - and, to be honest, it involved a good deal of self analysis - but it soon expanded beyond specific people and people in general to finally focus solely on the visual arts. It was at this point that I began to wonder why our reaction or response can sometimes seem completely at odds with the nature of the stimulus with which we are confronted. The more I thought about it, the more obvious it became that many people react to external stimuli in ways that are accepted as being intellectually 'correct', while failing to display an emotional reaction or response to the same stimuli.

An example of this type of response, or lack of *genuine* response, is a group of people standing in front of a piece of abstract art. Uncertain as to whether they should *like* or *dislike* the artwork, and not wanting to appear ignorant by responding in the wrong way, some of these people will let themselves be totally guided by their intellect and will avoid making a response. If they decide to comment on the work, having deduced that the general consensus of opinion is that the work lacks merit, or, on the other hand, that it rivals the work of an artist like, for example, Jackson Pollock, they may tailor their comments accordingly. At no point does the visual stimulus (the artwork) actually appear to connect with their emotions. Yet these very same people can respond, without problem, to an abstract pattern in a floor covering or a curtain material where there are no intellectual stipulations as to how they should or should not respond.

In other words, I became increasingly aware that many people are obstructed by their intellect to the point where they are incapable of having an honest spontaneous response. Underlying this dilemma is the fact that *some* art critics, experts and teachers set their own subjective opinions and observations as intellectual benchmarks that then determine how art should be assessed. In far too many cases, these assessment frameworks have a tendency to favour an intellectual response at the cost of an undiluted soul-stirring response.

Being a visual person, I set about creating an image of the problem in the form of a diagram, and it was in this way that my monad came into being.

Beginning with a circle to symbolize the whole person, I placed the emotions and spirituality (or the soul) in the centre. Around the edge of the circle, I then placed the five senses: sight, hearing, taste, touch and smell, and I devoted the area between the band of senses and the emotional, spiritual core to the intellect. Although imagination and will are important facets of this core, they can, to varying extents, be influenced by the intellect, and, with this in mind, they have been placed at the very edge of the spiritual centre.

The Ultimate Monad

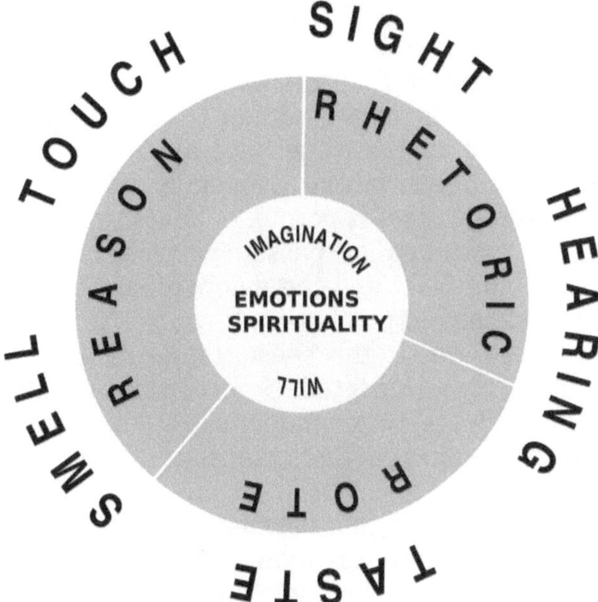

The monad, therefore, has an emotional, spiritual core surrounded by the intellect, which in turn is surrounded by the five senses. The senses collect information from the world around us and send this information through the intellect and, hopefully, into the very core of the monad.

It is the band of intellect between the emotions or feelings and the five senses – comprising reason, rote and rhetoric - which can often block our ability to have valid emotional responses. When our response is thwarted in this way, our ability to truly appreciate art is impacted negatively. An unobstructed inner response is pivotal to an honest appreciation of everything, especially art.

When the intellect is porous – that is to say, when there are openings or passageways between the senses, the intellect and the emotions – information from the senses passes easily through the intellect to the inner core. As this sensory information moves through the band of intellect, it can collect stored insights and facts, which in many cases may actually heighten or enhance the resulting emotional response.

For the person with a permeable intellect, his or her spiritual, intuitive response to a specific painting or to an impressive display of storm clouds may be intensified by the knowledge he or she has gathered on the particular artist or on the activity of clouds.

On the other hand, a sealed-off, impermeable intellect prevents contact between external stimuli and the emotional core and, as a result, prohibits a pure response. If the person looking at the painting, or the storm clouds, has an impervious intellect, then all the sensory information collected from the painting or the clouds will remain caught in the band of intellect and will not be able to reach the emotional core. The person may be able to analyse and appreciate both the painting and the clouds on an intellectual, rational level but will fail to connect with either on a more spiritual, sensitive level.

At the beginning of life, the newborn baby can be seen as possessing a core of feelings and an outer ring of senses. This outer ring, like the waving fronds of some exotic sea plant, collects innumerable impressions from the external world and delivers them to the baby's inner core for response. For example, a loud voice or a barrage of visuals may cause the baby to cry, while gentle music or a soft blanket may calm him/her. The band of intellect is present but has very little part to play; the baby responds to its senses on the basis of its feelings without any intellectual input.

However, it does not take long before the intellect begins to make itself noticed. A good example is the baby crying for attention. Having cried once or twice, or even three times, and having received some kind of reassuring attention on each occasion, the baby equates crying with receiving attention. Once the baby begins to put this into practice, that is to say, crying simply in order to receive attention, it can be said that he/she is beginning to use that part of the intellect devoted to rhetoric.

Initially the intellect is only made up of rhetoric, but as the baby grows and begins to remember things and is able to repeat responses to stimuli, rhetoric divides into rhetoric and rote. Later, by natural progression, reason also takes its place in the band of intellect. The intellect now includes rhetoric, rote and reason (and one can only hope that it is always reason that dominates).

By this stage, the child has moved into what I have chosen to call the *Ultimate Monad* – the monad with a porous band of intellect between the exterior senses and the inner feelings or emotions – which, during the years between childhood and adulthood, should reach a state of perfection.

However, for those who become focused on the *why* and the *how* behind external stimuli, the band of intellect will eventually lose its porosity. These people will become less and less able to respond emotionally, and as a result the monad itself will be less than perfect. In such cases, where the monad becomes sealed off, the information, ideas and opinions, which comprise the intellect, will often offer sufficient stimulation and satisfaction, and there may be no realization of what is being missed on an inner, spiritual level.

In other words, when a person consciously or subconsciously allows the intellect to process all external stimuli without allowing the senses free access to the emotions, the intellect becomes an impervious band obstructing contact between the senses and the inner core. The open passages close up and everything the person sees, hears, smells, touches or even tastes is vetted by the intellect, usually resulting in no emotional response or in a pseudo-emotional response that has been created in the rote section of the intellect.

Many people with sealed-off monads are highly intelligent, and among them I would place some of our greatest thinkers. They have formidable minds, but any connection with their spirituality or feelings is often greatly restricted – responses and conclusions being made on the basis of intellect and reasoning powers, not on the basis of the emotions and imagination.

The Sealed-off Monad

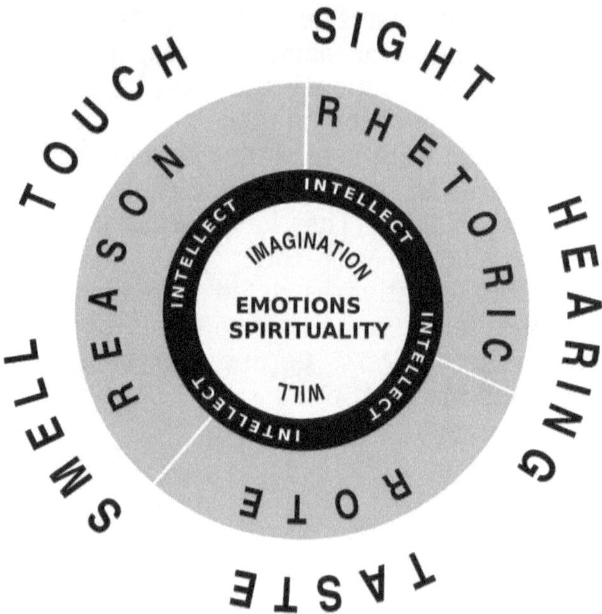

When it comes to the creative arts, people with
sealed-off monads - highly intelligent or otherwise
- may, for example, agree that a certain artwork is

brilliant on the basis of what has been written concerning either the artwork or the person who
created it, but they may choose to ignore an
imaginative or exciting piece of art by an unknown
artist about whom they *know* absolutely nothing.

They are the people who prefer to discuss the
technicalities of the painting or the sculpture or
the piece of music as though the *way* the paint is
applied to the canvas or the notes are written on
the paper is of more importance than *what* the paint
or notes are actually conveying. They are the
people who are more or less completely controlled
by their intellects.

The creative arts, which naturally demand an
open link between the senses and the inner core of
feelings and imagination, are bound to suffer when
creativity is intellectualized. Many people who talk
and write about the creative process are more than
often people connected with the creative arts, but
the pressure on them to submit to accepted
intellectual frameworks can often cause them to
analyse and interpret artworks from a purely
intellectual perspective, which, in turn, can lead to
a sealing off or a stifling of their own intuitive responses.

WHAT IS ART?

In order to explain how the monad relates to art, I must first define what I mean by art. Art is *anything* that triggers an emotional or soul response; it is, in fact, anything that penetrates, or bypasses, the intellect to connect with a feeling or stir up the imagination. Poetically speaking, it can be described as the bolt of magic lightning that, when sensed, fires the soul. A response to a piece of art, be it a painting, a sculpture, a piece of music or even nature itself, should never be determined by intellectual consideration or assessment, but should always spring directly from the emotions or from that which we might call the soul.

Of all the creative art forms, music is probably the one most easily enjoyed by the greatest number of people, while painting and sculpture, although enjoyed by many people, can sometimes present problems for genuine, intellect-free appreciation. Yet, in spite of this, when most people hear the word *art,* the very first image that comes to mind is that of a painting or a sculpture.

While many people have no problem enjoying 'photographic' paintings or 'lifelike' sculptures, their enjoyment and appreciation can be for all the wrong reasons. In many cases their response to the art-work is not at all spiritual or intuitive, but it is an intellectual appreciation of how clever the artist must have been to have painted, or sculpted, such an incredible likeness. On the other hand, when it comes to music, which in many ways is the most abstract art form of all, these very same people often *do* experience a genuine spiritual, emotional response. In stark contrast to the painting or the sculpture, the music does not have to sound like, or resemble, anything in nature or the man-made environment in order to be acceptable.

If we are to fully enjoy and appreciate any of the visual arts as they deserve to be both enjoyed and appreciated, our eye must first relinquish its un-necessary dependency on the intellect. Too often, images entering through the eye are waylaid by the intellect before they have a chance to reach the inner sentient core. This path must be cleared so that a direct eye-to-soul (or eye-to-emotion) con-nection is possible.

When you are able to *see* in the same beautifully relaxed manner that you can *hear,* you stand on the threshold of many exciting visual experiences. You are then in a position to observe nature as the French Impressionists saw her a century ago: a world of colours, shapes and tones – a vision that does not need to be labelled and/or analysed in order to be enjoyed. It is only then that the wonderful beauty of the abstract in nature can reverberate in its own right, completely independent of the intellect.

Art, no matter the medium, and no matter to which of the senses it may relate, can be good or bad, desirable or undesirable, true or counterfeit, beautiful or ugly, joyful or sorrowful, fine or commercial. Consequently, subjects and experiences as diverse as religion, love, birth, death, war, violence and nature itself, must cover an enormous range of feelings and emotions, from the very positive to the very negative, all of which are capable of inciting a soul-stirring response in the viewer or the recipient. If something – a play, a painting, a piece of music, an art installation – fires the soul, either positively or negatively, then, whether it looks like our preconceived idea of it or not, it has to be art.

The many negative feelings that can be stirred up by graffiti, violence, ugliness and decay are *also* intense responses to external stimuli, and we must, therefore, start by dividing art into what we might call the *desirable* and the *undesirable*, keeping in mind that *undesirable* art is just as much art as the *desirable*.

In other words, the bolt firing the soul can be positive, negative or even something in between. The only important thing from the point of view of art is that the action results in a heartfelt response.

Only the end result, the effect, counts: how it was produced or what caused it to be is totally irrelevant. Too often a person viewing a piece of art will ask: 'But what is it all about? What does it mean?' Such questions will often be posed by the intellect when the person knows nothing about the artwork, and there is a fear of possibly appearing uneducated. In some cases, there may even be a fear of being deceived into liking something that actually means nothing at all. It is not the meaning that is important, it is the response.

Whether an artist is merely throwing indiscriminate colours on a canvas, for whatever reason, or whether he/she is having an authentic intuitive response to the creative process is completely irrelevant. The effect on the recipient or the viewer is the only criterion that matters. If the canvas with unordered blobs of colour results in a deep inner response in just one single viewer, then it must be called a work of art.

Inasmuch as art excites and kindles the soul it can be called 'soul power', and this power can lie latent in the paint and the shapes on the canvas, in the words of the poem, in the sounds of the waterfall, in the smoothness of the rock... until someone receptive to its message acknowledges its existence. Then it stirs itself, and passes unnoticed through the intellect to energize the soul.

ART AND THE MONAD

In the mid 1980s, I attended a workshop on the Gestalt method of psychology, the central principle of which is that the mind perceives external stimuli as a whole and not as a sum of disconnected parts. A lecturer from one of Brisbane's universities was also attending the workshop, and in one of the breaks we got talking not only about the workshop but also about related subjects. During our conversation, I mentioned my monad and how I felt that it was a symbolic representation of the way we respond to external stimuli and, more especially, the way these responses affect our appreciation of art. The lecturer was immediately interested, and after I had spent some minutes explaining how the diagram worked, he asked for a copy.

I am aware of Jung's use of the circle symbol to signify a safe place and of the Buddhist practice of using concentric circles to symbolize the stages of perfection; however, my monad, though based on a circular form, is unrelated to the circles of either Jung or the Buddhists. Instead it is the result of my own thought processes, spanning a period of more than forty years. That said, I am aware that certain facets of my thinking, indeed, all of them for that matter, are not necessarily new; in fact, nothing can ever be completely new as all thoughts spring from the same universal source and are consequently recycled. We are all merely conduits for the thoughts and the ideas that emanate from that source.

An example of this is the monad pattern, which must have rested somewhere within me for many years. Even though I did not become aware of it as a reality until the 1980s, I had subconsciously been using the techniques it implied since the 1950s.

This is the only explanation I have for children in my art classes so readily accepting the importance of the spiritual, imaginative response, or for adults in my evening classes – who were already exhibiting sealed-off monads – being able to unlock their emotional responses. Such positive reactions from children and students should underline how important it is for teachers – not only art teachers – to fully grasp the concept behind the monad, that is to say, the importance of keeping passageways open between external stimuli and the inner, spiritual core.

Unfortunately, there is a lot of rhetoric used in the art world, and much of it comes from art critics and historians who already have sealed-off monads.

When I was at art school in the late 1940s, I studied art history and art appreciation under Mary

Packer Harris, who, although passionate about all forms of visual art, had a tendency to intellectualize the subject. She devoted much time to the composition of paintings: the use of lines and shapes, the arrangement of objects, contrast and balance... elements that were all important from a technical perspective but which, in actual fact, had nothing to do with a *true* appreciation of art. I can remember becoming completely focused on the *construction* of paintings without even considering the emotional response that the painting might or might not evoke. I fully accept that it is necessary to learn and master different techniques, but techniques on their own do not make art, do they? For the artist, art comes into being when the picture takes over, a point at which he/she enters the realm of the emotions and spirituality.

HOW TO TRULY APPRECIATE ART

In order to fully appreciate art through an unadulterated emotional response, it is first necessary to penetrate the band of intellect that lies between the senses and the central core of spiritual awareness. It is the intellect that demands explanations and persists in examining everything sensed. Only by bypassing or ignoring the intellect is it possible to experience a genuine soul response.

Any response to art, no matter to which of the five senses it may appeal, will be extremely frustrated as long as we focus on our intellect's concern as to where the art object came from, what it actually is or how it was produced. The situation becomes much worse if we are afraid of being fooled, looking ridiculous or appearing ignorant. We may, for example, have a horror of saying that we like something that turns out to be the work of an amateur or, heaven forbid, a child. It is important that we can ignore the concerns and the structures imposed by the intellect and allow ourselves to experience an honest inner response.

Religion is a good example of how it is possible to ignore the intellect while responding emotionally.

An acceptance of religion is usually based on a willingness not to question (intellectually) but to have faith (emotionally). Religion scored a high spiritual or soul response until some people began asking for proof in rational terms. The result was that the great intellectual atheists appeared on the scene and consequently destroyed religion not only for themselves but for many others as well. There could be no scientific proof, and there never can be. Like religion, the essence of art is intangible and will always remain so.

It is important to understand that appreciation of art is *always* a direct sensory perception-to-soul happening. There does not have to be any prior intellectual knowledge about the art object being appreciated – the object is all that is needed for a sincere intuitive response based on feelings. There is no need for any explanations, and there is definitely no need to intellectualize the response.

In conclusion, it can, therefore, be seen that an appreciation of the world around us (in general) and art in all its forms (in particular) is completely reliant on external stimuli – visual, auditory, gustatory, olfactory, tactile – being able to penetrate or bypass the intellect and reach the emotions. The size and/or thickness of the intellect has very little to do with this process, but the density of the intellect is extremely important. When the intellect is permeable, external stimuli can pass through it to instigate an authentic intuitive response.

An old deserted factory building is not much more than an eyesore, and an abstract painting, composed of irregular segments of colour, merely an intellectual challenge when the building and the painting are regarded through a sealed-off monad; however, if the passages between these visual stimuli and the recipient's inner core are open, then the building and the painting will be able to speak directly to the feelings, the imagination and the soul. The deserted building will be appreciated for its wondrous collection of shapes, textures and colours as they fuse together to create new shapes and new realities. The segments of colour in the painting, without any need to justify their existence intellectually, will be able to trigger a natural, uncorrupted response based on feelings – a response that can be either positive or negative but at all times genuine.

In our relationship with the external world, it is important, at all times, to keep the passages open between what our senses are perceiving and our inner spiritual core. The three parts of the monad: the emotional core, the intellect and the external senses should exist as a harmonious whole; a sealed-off monad where the intellect is completely in charge can only lead to a life half lived.

AFTERWORD

Living life, for every individual, is an art form in essence. In communicating with others we adopt whatever channel of the many in which we operate that is most appropriate for the person/persons involved.

Intellectual honesty is a rare commodity, but, at first meeting Diane Eklund-Āboliņš, almost a decade ago, I felt a connection in a channel of a spiritual kind: the one essential to the arts.

The ideas about art and the psyche first emerged for me in my 50th year of life, but all attempts to express in terms for others to accept have failed. Now in my 87th year, this wonderful revelation of finding, in Diane, a conduit through which to share with others these ideas through her talents, both as a writer and visual artist, brings the ultimate joy.

This entire work, from cover design through writing and formatting, is the sole execution of Diane, who has been able to tune in so precisely with my thoughts to produce what I hope may be of benefit to others in the society in which we serve.

Throughout the time of presenting this idea over the last 35 years, I have always explained that I used the word *rhetoric* as a euphemism for *bullshit,* but in deference to Diane's professionalism this colloquial term does not appear in the essay.

Finally I must express my sincere appreciation to Diane, for her perseverance, and to Andris Abolins, a professional portrait photographer, for the image that appears inside the front cover.

KLC
West Gosford, Australia
June 2016